I0424815

The American Military Advisor:

Dealing with Senior Foreign Officials in the
Islamic World

Art and promotional text (c) Booklife 2010
ISBN 978-1-105-81077-0

This publication is subject to Title 17, United States
Code, Sections 101 and 105. It is in the public domain
and may not be copyrighted.

The views expressed in this report are those of the author and do not necessarily reflect the official policy or position of the Department of the Army, the Department of Defense, or the U.S. Government. This report is cleared for public release; distribution is unlimited.

*****

The author is grateful to all his military and civilian colleagues who offered comment and advice on this effort. They have served as diplomats, soldiers, and advisors in critical times and in a wide variety of conflict zones, and the impact of their role is seldom fully appreciated. His thanks goes especially to Ambassador (Ret.) Ron Neumann, Ambassador (Ret.) Marisa Lino, Ambassador (Ret.) John Limbert, Ambassador Mike Malinowski, Professor Richard Smyth, Professor Clementine Fujimura, Professor Hekmat Sadat, Lieutenant Colonel Mark Drabik, Colonel Michael G. Clark, Colonel Mike Moon, Colonel Tom Pope, Ms. Susan Merrill, and Mr. Bruce Boevers.

*****

Comments pertaining to this report are invited and should be forwarded to: Director, Strategic Studies Institute, U.S. Army War College, 122 Forbes Ave, Carlisle, PA 17013-5244.

CONTENTS

Foreword vii

Biographical Sketch of the Author............................ix

Summary xi

I. Introduction 1

II. What Is an Advisor? 6

    Definition 6

    Differences in Perception..................................8

    Differences in Time Frame 11

    The Local Calendar Takes Precedence..........14

III. Selection and Qualifications of the Advisor....17

    Assigning the Right Person or the

    Right Team 17

    Rank, Gender, and Age 19

IV. The Advisor's Tools for Success 22

    Professional, Academic,

    and Life Experience 22

    The Advisor's Personality 26

    Personal Flexibility 27

    Knowing the Local Culture 28

    Knowing American Culture

    and History 34

    Knowing the Terrain 35

    The Hypocrisy Factor 37

V. The Language Problem 40

    Use of Interpreters 41

    Using "Basic" English 45

    Using a Third Language 47

    Understanding What Is Heard and What

    Is Said...48

    Non-verbal Communication 51

VI.   The Office as Battle Space 52

       The First Who in Who's Who 52

       Foreign Officials' Sources of Income 55

       Local Perception of Government Service......57

       The Trap of Personally Identifying with

       Foreign Officials 59

VII. Other Players on the Field 63

       The U.S. Government Writ Large 63

       The Country Team 65

       Other International Players 66

       The Domestic Constituency 67

       The Media 67

VIII. Military Assistance Available

to the Advisor 70

       Essential Services 70

       Personal Risk: A Cost-Benefit Analysis 74

IX.   Preparation and Coordination—

Approaching the Job...76

       The Preparation Checklist 76

X.   Departing the Country 81

       Endnotes 83

FOREWORD

This publication is the first in a new series, entitled PKSOI Papers, being published by the Strategic Studies Institute and the U.S. Army's Peacekeeping and Stability Operations Institute. This paper will be followed on a periodic basis with publications focused on peacekeeping and stability operations. Future papers will include scholarly articles on issues of interest to civilian and military practitioners from the international community, U.S. Government, and nongovernmental organizations. Our intent is to maintain the focus at the strategic and interagency level in an effort to inform individuals responsible for establishing policy as well as senior level practitioners of stability operations.

This introductory paper concerns the role of the American military advisor. Military officers have frequently been called upon to serve as advisors to foreign officials and to play seminal roles in the political and development realms overseas. Lawrence of Arabia's work with Arabs attempting to build a nation-state during World War I and the role of military advisors in post-World War II Japan and Germany are well-known examples of the impact that officers can have on political evolution and strategic success in areas of conflict. In today's Iraq and Afghanistan, the role of the military advisor has expanded greatly, and the relationships established by American officers at the strategic level with local Governors, Cabinet Members and other civilian policymakers are easily as important as any strictly military officer to military officer role. The advisory function traditionally has not been part of military preparation and training, yet the consequences of failure or success on the part of

American military advisors are far-reaching for the United States.

Based on the experience of diplomats and military officers who have served in many zones of conflict, and whose duties meant daily interaction with senior foreign officials, this guide describes the preparations that an advisor should make, illustrates the questions he should ask, and explains the political and cultural complexities that affect his mission. Although most of the examples are drawn from Islamic countries, the precepts and advice apply broadly.

JOHN A. KARDOS
Colonel, U.S. Army
Director
Peacekeeping and Stability
Operations Institute

DOUGLAS C. LOVELACE, JR.
Director
Strategic Studies Institute

BIOGRAPHICAL SKETCH OF THE AUTHOR

MICHAEL J. METRINKO is a retired Foreign Service Officer with extensive experience in the Islamic world, a region with which he has been dealing for almost 40 years. He was a Peace Corps volunteer for 5 years in Turkey and Iran, and State Department assignments took him back to Turkey and Iran, as well as Poland, Syria, Yemen and Israel for another 14 years. Mr. Metrinko was a member of the Tehran Embassy staff taken hostage in 1979 and spent 14 months as a prisoner in Iran. His assignments in Washington DC, included 2 years as Deputy Director of the Iran-Iraq Desk and 3 years as an Office Director in the Bureau of Population, Refugees, and Migration, where he had oversight responsibility for refugee programs in Europe, South Asia, and the Middle East. Mr. Metrinko returned to active government service after the events of September 11, 2001, with assignments to Yemen, Iraq, and 4 years in Afghanistan at U.S. and North Atlantic Treaty Organization provincial reconstruction teams (PRTs) and at the U.S. Embassy in Kabul. His last posting was as the Advisor on Parliamentary Affairs for the U.S. Embassy in Kabul, where he spent more than 1 1/2 years dealing directly with the new Afghan National Assembly. Mr. Metrinko now serves as Ministry Reform Advisor at the U.S. Army Peacekeeping and Stability Operations Institute, based at Carlisle Barracks, Pennsylvania.

SUMMARY

The American Military Advisor: Dealing with Senior Foreign Officials in the Islamic World is a comprehensive guide for American military officers assigned as advisors to regional officials in places very different from the United States. Starting with a definition of terms and a brief description of the advisory role, it brings the reader into today's Islamic political and social context, pointing out the complexities inherent in the advisory position, as well as the tools an advisor must use in order to perform successfully. The precepts and examples in the text are based on the personal experiences of a number of diplomats and military officers who have seen extensive service in the Islamic world and in many conflict zones. The text is not a simple list of do's and don'ts, but rather it explains the type of questions that an advisor should ask, the preparations he should make, and the characteristics he should display in order to complete his advisory mission successfully.

The advisory role is at best loosely defined in military career terms, and realities on the ground further complicate the advisory mission. These include differences in American and foreign perception of the advisory position, differences in the way Americans and host country officials view time lines, the impact of the local calendar on the advisor's work, and the importance of cultural adaptation and intellectual openness. In the end, establishing personal rapport with a host country official is the basis for success as an advisor, and the qualities in an advisor's personality that allow for such a relationship are difficult to quantify.

Assigning advisors poses a challenge to the military personnel system because of age, gender, and cultural values in the Islamic world, and the characteristics that help make an advisor successful—his personality, openness to new cultures, and flexibility in dealing in uncharted areas—are not normally considered by the military selection process. A good advisor's skill set includes language ability, cross-cultural adaptation and knowledge, and a solid foundation in American history and politics, as well as expertise in his particular military field. Normally an advisor will be partnered with an interpreter, and understanding this relationship is vital, just as studying and understanding the new terrain to which the advisor is assigned and the foreign officials with whom he will be working. How the host country views the United States and how its citizens regard their own officials affect the advisor's role.

The advisor is never alone in his new environment, and a variety of other players, from the American Embassy, international organizations, the media, nongovernment agencies, and the local populace affect the advisory mission as well. Understanding the roles played by this variety of actors is essential to the advisor, since they can provide support and cooperation as well as hinder his mission.

Although difficult to define and open to change as time at the job passes, the advisor's role is nonetheless essential in today's American political and military environment. The advisor is placed squarely in the host country's decisionmaking process, and his skill and ability impact directly on overall American interests in the Islamic world.

THE AMERICAN MILITARY ADVISOR: DEALING WITH SENIOR FOREIGN OFFICIALS IN THE ISLAMIC WORLD

> Another reality the uniformed forces must accept cultur-ally is that, like it or not, until further notice the U.S. gov-ernment has decided that the military largely owns the job of nation-building. Although the Nation, its political leadership, and its military have routinely dismissed this mission since the end of the Cold War, we have repeat-edly decided to commit our national power to it. Today the U.S. military is the only national organization able to conduct some of the most critical tasks associated with re-building war-torn or failed nations.

> Lieutenant General Peter Chiarelli
> *Military Review*, September-October 2007

I. INTRODUCTION

The events of September 11, 2001 (9/11) and subsequent U.S. military and political operations in Afghanistan and Iraq have changed American military-civil relations throughout the region, generating relationships between American military officers and senior foreign officials in ways never envisioned in traditional training manuals. American military officers now serve as advisors to senior foreign officials in Afghanistan, Iraq, and many other countries. There is little in military doctrine that addresses such relationships, or in regular training that equips officers to serve as advisors to foreign Cabinet Ministers, Governors and, at times, even Heads of State. The problem is compounded by profound differences in background, culture, and mindset between American officers and foreign officials.

1

The role of advisor is a complex one, and not easy to categorize. Even the terminology commonly used to describe the function is not perfect. For example, although often used in discussion, the word "mentor" is not a good choice to describe an American officer's advisory role vis-à-vis a senior foreign official, since mentoring implies a relationship between a superior and someone younger, or inferior in status and rank. In the world of strategic partnerships, and in a setting where expertise, experience, social status, political rank, and financial resources can be more heavily weighted on the foreign official's side, "mentor" is a misnomer. Even the word "advisor" can be misleading, but there is, however, no perfect word to use. The function goes far beyond merely advising a foreign official on military tactics or logistics, often spilling into the political sphere and blurring the lines between the officer's core duties and the responsibilities of State Department, U.S. Agency for International Development (USAID), and other civilian officials. It touches the realm of nation-building, affecting the relationship that the foreign official has with the American government, and the relationship between his country and the United States. The advisory role can bring the American officer into political realms that traditionally are distant from his reach, and be more of a learning experience for the American than it is for the senior local official. As such, it has value in itself.

Advising foreign officials in a conflict or post-conflict situation is not a new phenomenon for military officers, and the classic example of "Lawrence of Arabia" comes immediately to mind. American military officers have had such responsibilities in post-World War II in Europe and Japan, and more recently in Korea, Vietnam, Haiti, Bosnia, Kosovo, Afghanistan, and Iraq, but in general, their responsibilities have been at the tactical level. There have been American advisors at the highest levels, particularly in Germany and Japan, when high-level restructuring of those governments was done by American military officers, but unfortunately this competency within the military structure has diminished or not been formalized and passed to succeeding generations. Yet mid- and senior-level officers have a productive and often vital role to play as advisors in a wide variety of areas.

In the post-9/11 world, an advisory position at the political and strategic level in the Islamic world can have great and immediate consequence for U.S. interests, and can make the American advisor a prime figure in the decisionmaking process of foreign leaders. The advisor is as likely to be dealing with a civilian counterpart as he is with a foreign military officer, and the range of duties will go far beyond mere military tasks. The position has become a critical one in today's world, where stability, peacekeeping, and obtaining civil support are considered equally important to kinetic offensive and defensive operations, and where "nation-building" has become a de facto and integral part of the military mission.

The guidance herein is based predominantly on experience in the Islamic world of the Middle East and Afghanistan, in areas that are generally (but not completely) Muslim, conservative, and very traditional. These are also countries in flux, with rapidly changing political and military realities that pose a challenge to local mores and tradition, and affect the way that America is viewed by the populace. All of the countries cited are strategically important to the United States, and even routine events and decisions in these places can directly affect America's security and political interests. Media portrayal of events in these countries can resonate throughout a large part of the Islamic world, and the American military advisor's role can be pivotal in determining policy and affecting the country's development. While most examples cited in this handbook are based on service in the Islamic word, many of the principles and lessons have universal application.

Even within the Islamic world, great disparities exist in socio-economic conditions, traditions, and behavior. Some countries are wealthy, with national income guaranteed by natural resources and business development, and some are so poor that their very survival as political entities can be at risk. Sunni Muslims differ from Shi'ite Muslims, and each of these major groups has internal ethnic and religious components that differ from one another as well. Life in Turkey is quite different from Yemen, and Algeria is not the same as Indonesia. The sophisticated Shi'ite Persian socialite in Tehran may have nothing in common with a Sunni tribesman from the Maghreb, and a young Pashtun Afghan member of the Wahabbi-influenced Taliban lives in a very different spiritual world than a moderate Sunni Turkish businessman from Istanbul. A wealthy Arab Muslim entrepreneur from Dubai with a household staff of Indian or Filipino servants lives very differently than a Bedouin nomad.

This diverse world is often further complicated by the presence of large Christian and other non-Muslim religious communities which claim long histories and economic and social prominence, by large western expatriate communities, and by a wide variety of domestic tribal and ethnic groups whose traditions color their customs and their behavior. This presence and role of sub-cultures and diverse ethnic, cultural, and regional groups are not unique to the Islamic world, but can be found in almost every society and country.

Although Muslim countries and cultures differ from one another, and methods of approach will change depending on locale, there are certain generalities that define the relationship of an advisor to foreign officials in this world:

1. *The advisor can assist and consult, but he cannot command. It is, after all, not his house and not his own country. He is a counselor, not a colonial administrator.*

2. *The advisor should have expertise, but he does not have the last word. Policy direction and limits are set by his commander and by the American Ambassador, and policy will shift to conform to political shifts within the United States, the local population, and among local elected officials. Final decisionmaking is in the foreign official's hands.*

3. *The advisor must cooperate with other players, both foreign and American. Working alone does not mean being alone. The other players can enhance — or dilute — the officer's influence.*

4. *The advisor must be a true American, but not an Ugly American. Whatever his own religious and political convictions, the advisor must show respect for local culture and tradition to be successful. He is not a judge.*

5. *The advisor should not be a hypocrite. If he is not prepared to live by his own advice, he should not expect others to follow it.*

6. *The advisor should be humble. He should always remember that his audience may not have his resources, his background of living in a peaceful, orderly society, or his confidence in a good future and a guaranteed pension following retirement.*

7. *And finally, the advisor must be helpful, but also credible. He should never promise what he cannot deliver.*

II. WHAT IS AN ADVISOR?

The academic definition of the term "advisor" changes in practice because of historic and regional differences, and the advisor's role and responsibilities are ultimately determined on the ground. The American and his counterpart bring their own cultural differences and life experiences to bear on their roles.

Definition.

The dictionary definition of "advisor" is succinct: An "advisor" is a "person who offers advice, especially in an official or professional capacity." And "advice" is "opinion from one not immediately concerned as to what could, or should be done about a problem." In the present political and military world, however, the role of advisor is a complicated, sophisticated, and sensitive one, usually involving dangerous environments and the potential for great success or even greater loss.

In today's reality, the American advisor serves an essential role. A U.S. military advisor for a senior foreign official is part of an American military structure with a defined chain of command and clearly delineated responsibilities. His assignment will change with circumstance, but is usually to advise the official on military and other matters, to act as liaison between the U.S. military hierarchy and the senior official, and to effect action by the official which will be in the interests of the United States. How he does his task will depend on his personality and that of the senior official whom he is advising, on conditions in the country, and on American domestic political considerations. The U.S. presence in the host country, the resources the United States brings to meet the country's needs, and the security and political relationship the United States offers may be vital to the country's survival and prosperity.

The advisor interprets the American viewpoint to the official and helps him avoid misunderstandings that can affect both countries. He can reach back to the U.S. government on the official's behalf to harness and help direct resources — in training, material, and financial terms — that will have great impact on the country's stability and prosperity. It is only when he learns to trust his American advisor that a foreign official, in quiet, private conversations, may ask the American to explain the personalities or the real status of the American political figures the official must deal with, or ask advice on the best way to approach the U.S. government bureaucracy on official matters. By being sensitive to the official's concerns, and by giving credible and honest advice when both can speak in full confidence, the advisor directly affects the two countries' relations.

The foreign official is also in a chain of command, and it is possible that U.S. political and military priorities differ from those of the official's service, agency, or country. The official may also have advisors and consultants from other countries and other organizations, and his actions may be affected by a range of factors that far outweigh the American's advice.

The advisor's success depends both on himself as well as external factors over which he has no control. As Lieutenant Colonel Mark Grdovic notes in his article "The Advisory Challenge,"

> the amount of influence an advisor attains will be
> directly proportional to the sum of three factors: the
> rapport between the advisor and the host-nation
> commander or counterpart; the credibility of the
> individual advisor; and the perception by host-nation
> forces of the continued value of the relationship.[1]

Ultimately, the core skills necessary for a successful advisory role are the same from the tactical to the strategic level, involving the combination of personality, credibility, and perception of value. These factors hold true for the junior noncommissioned officers (NCOs) and junior company grade officers assigned to provide training to the lowest level of foreign army recruits, as well as to the general who is sitting in a meeting with a foreign head of state.

Differences in Perception.

The concept of the advisor's role may be very different in foreign versus U.S. military eyes, and the advisor should understand that he may not always be welcome. A senior foreign official may not see any need for an American advisor, no matter what agreements have been made between his president and the American military commander or ambassador. The result may be the isolation of the advisor, simply sending him off to a remote desk with no access to the official's person or activities. The advisor must remember that the perception of American influence is a two-edged sword. If the foreign official is personally sensitive to his country's weakened status or to the implication that the U.S. advisor is a "watchdog" or a "spy" with authority over the official's activities, he will resent the American's presence, and others in the office will be certain to feed the official's paranoia by slanted reports of what the American is doing and who he is seeing.

The advisor must be sensitive to the burden of historic precedence. In Afghanistan, for example, anyone serving as a military advisor today might remind Afghans of the onerous presence and heavy hands of Soviet military advisors in the 1980s, when the country was occupied by force by the Union of Soviet Socialist Republics (USSR). While the North American Treaty Organization (NATO) and American presence in Afghanistan today is a far cry from the Soviet occupation, a significant percent of the population, including senior members of the government and power structure, object to *any* foreign military presence. For this reason, an official who utilizes a foreign advisor may be regarded by some of his countrymen as a collaborator with a foreign occupying force.

*****

Local reaction to the presence and activities of American soldiers can range from welcoming to the intense and hostile, even from ostensibly "friendly" counterpart officials. In the summer of 2002, an Afghan who was driving two American officers in Kabul tried to evade a police checkpoint at the officers' instruction. Forced to a stop by the local police, he was pulled out of the vehicle. When he explained that he was driving American officials, the police called him a "pimp for the Americans," slapped him, then finally let him reenter the car.

*****

In the past few several years, many Afghan and Iraqi civilians have been threatened or even murdered by insurgents, with the reasons cited being their cooperation with the United States. Collaboration and even simple employment are often viewed as treason.

*****

The American advisor must take care not to let himself be regarded as just another person who has come to pass out gifts in order to curry favor. He must not be regarded as simply a source of material assistance, supplies, high tech presents, and trips abroad under the rubric of training. In resource-strapped Afghanistan, for example, local and even senior officials became accustomed to requesting telephones, office furniture, office supplies, security accessories and equipment of all sorts, vehicles, and a wide variety of other items from Provincial Reconstruction Team (PRT) commanders, American officials, and other foreign visitors and donors. On many occasions, the Afghans would request the same items from multiple sources.

The advisor must look at himself through local eyes and the local culture. If the American officer's "can do" attitude is too highly developed, he may just seem ill-mannered and abrasive to the official and his staff, who often operate at a different tempo than that in U.S. military circles. If he appears to be too young and lacking in authority, the American may be regarded simply as a decorative foreign staff aide who tags along to add luster of the official's entourage.

*****

Age is important in many parts of the traditional Islamic world. For example, the term "white beard" is commonly

10

used in Afghanistan as a term of respect, implying that only someone who has grown old has experience and expertise. Tribal and village elders are the source of advice and authority, not the younger generation, and young men attending a major meeting or assembly are expected to sit silently and listen to the older generation.

*****

The American advisor and the senior foreign official will come to their own understanding of an appropriate scope of responsibility and access. The initial arrangement will probably change over time. There are no fixed parameters, and personalities and local reality will be the deciding factors in determining what the advisor is supposed to do and how he will do it.

**Differences in Time Frame:
When "Tomorrow" Really Means "Never."**

The senior foreign official and the American advisor may have very different concepts of the time necessary to complete an action. Some cultures do not place value on undue haste, and the smart advisor soon learns that "bukra" or "fardo" ("tomorrow" in Arabic and Farsi) or "inshallah" ("God willing" in Farsi/Dari/Turkish and Arabic) often mean that action has been relegated to some other time and place, but probably not any time soon or any place near.

Ignoring the local cultural concepts of timeliness will simply lead to frustration and ultimate failure for the advisor, and cause hidden discomfort and annoyance in his local counterpart in response to his frustration. In the Islamic world, religious holidays and daily prayer times will take precedence over scheduled meetings, and decisions may be made in loose gatherings with endless cups of tea rather than at official conference tables. A meeting may break, even at a critical moment, so that participants can pray as a group. Much of this world falls more into the "Haste Makes Waste" category rather than "The Early Bird Catches the Worm," with many meetings, programs, and social events only drifting towards a start when the senior official arrives.

*****

Everything takes time. A newly assigned advisor to an Afghan Cabinet Minister was at first unable to achieve his Commanding General's directive to be present in every meeting, obtain unlimited access to the Minister, and be able to get the Minister's schedule changed at a moment's notice. At first, the advisor was often relegated to a waiting room and only had limited entrée to the Minister's office. Within a few months, the advisor had gained the Minister's confidence to the point where he could sit in on all his meetings and could obtain immediate appointments for American VIP visitors. The advisor's impact on the Minister was publicly demonstrated when the foreign official asked the advisor to extend his tour, and the advisor was also accorded a medal through the Minister's efforts.

*****

An American officer assigned as an advisor normally knows how long his tour of duty will be. From the day that he arrives in-country, he hears a clock ticking off the days left in his assignment, and he may feel a subconscious compulsion to complete a check list of "things to do" in order to satisfy performance goals. His starting point for action is the date of his arrival at post. The U.S. government's fiscal year, his own evaluation report and upcoming meetings, official visits, American holidays, and the normal needs of his family in the United States can all be markers that affect his timing. Looking at his new environment, the advisor may feel that action is vital and should be immediate.

The foreign official, on the other hand, has a different view of time and a different perspective. His focus is indefinite, and he will not be rated on one year's performance. He has been a player in the long process that brought local conditions to their present state and assumes that he will be in power for a long time to come, so he generally will not share the American's sense of urgency. He probably does not share the Puritan work ethic either, and will see little reason to change his habits or his work environment in order to fit a foreigner's conception of what is appropriate. And the official has probably seen a large number of foreign advisors come and go, their names long since forgotten, and their presence leaving only minor or no impact on local conditions.

By the same token, the foreign official's tenure is ultimately uncertain. Because he owes his position to local politics in what is probably a volatile environment, he can be reassigned, disgraced, promoted on a whim, or assassinated. In Afghanistan or Iraq, any senior official will have had many friends and colleagues who were victims of political violence because of their leadership positions, and he himself may have been the target of assassination attempts or have sought to remove others that way in his rise to power. Despite all this, the official may possess a sense of personal surrender to such events or an acceptance of his danger that the advisor will find disconcerting. In the Islamic world, bowing to fate runs deeply throughout society. Risk aversion may be seen as cowardice and lack of honor by many local leaders.

The Local Calendar Takes Precedence.

The advisor should know the local calendar and understand the ramifications of holidays, local weekends, etc. These can change from country to country and even from region to region. For example, in Afghanistan and Iran, No Ruz, which falls during the third week of March, is widely celebrated as a happy, family-oriented holiday. Children are often given gifts, picnics are held outside, and many people pay congratulatory calls on their relatives, colleagues, and superiors. This can be a several-day period, and the savvy advisor will not try to arrange meetings for American delegations or expect his local colleagues to give up their family time. It would be akin to asking an American official to give up his Christmas.

In Shi'ite areas, the period commemorating Ashura, the day that the Prophet Muhammad's grandson Husayn was martyred at the Battle of Kerbala, can be especially sensitive. Shi'ite schools and mosques organize religious ceremonies that come out onto public streets, and may involve crowds of many thousands of men who are in a heightened state of religious emotion. If the local Shi'ite and Sunni communities do not have good relations, this can end up in violence and property destruction. It is not a time for foreign advisors to wander the local streets, arrange for visiting American delegations, or assume "business as usual." Even in the most peaceful areas, the focus is on religious martyrdom, with an increase of tension in the streets.

The period of Ramadan is especially difficult in all Muslim countries because many people fast, refraining from all food and drink, even water, during daylight hours. If Ramadan falls within the summer months in a hot climate, this can be debilitating for people who get no sustenance from dawn until dusk. It affects the entire society, from the traffic policeman to the young soldier to the Head of State. The fast is broken at the beginning of the evening, and many observers will wake up in the pre-dawn hours for a light meal. This means that the advisor's Muslim colleagues and visitors will be unusually tired from lack of sleep, that driving (especially as the evening hours approach and many people rush home to break their fast) can be erratic and dangerous, and that decisionmaking can be affected by frayed tempers and simple thirst, hunger, and exhaustion. Colleagues may arrive late to work, or depart very early.

Ramadan is also a time when social life becomes very active, with large numbers of banquets and gatherings held to celebrate the evening breaking of the fast. The advisor must take this into account, because during Ramadan (the dates change according to the lunar calendar) it will not be "business as usual." The incessant series of evening social events adds to the general exhaustion. The non-Muslim advisor is not expected to observe the fast personally, but should refrain, out of respect and consideration for his Muslim colleagues, from smoking, eating, or drinking in public or in front of his colleagues during daylight hours.

Just as other countries have their own holidays, do not expect foreign officials to take the American calendar into account. The Saturday/Sunday weekend, the anniversary of 9/11, Thanksgiving, Christmas and New Year's Eve may have no meaning at all to them, and the advisor should not take it personally when major American observances pass without any mention at all.

The bottom line is to know the local calendar well in advance, and refuse official American requests for meetings and visits that affect important observances. The local officials will be frustrated at not being able to properly host foreign delegations, and while they may put up a good front, everyone from the servant staff to the senior official will be annoyed, ill at ease, hungry, thirsty, tired, tense or just want to be home with their families. This will seriously damage the advisor's plans for a successful meeting or visit.

III. SELECTION AND QUALIFICATIONS OF THE ADVISOR

Proper selection of an advisor is complex, because the required skills and knowledge are intangible, and not those of the normal soldier. Knowledge of the human terrain, and the abilities to work independently in a foreign environment and to negotiate are vital traits. An advisor's personality and qualifications will be scrutinized and judged by his foreign counterparts who use different criteria than the U.S. military personnel system.

> Not only is the military situation strange, but the human milieu — the psychological and social context in which he works — is also foreign and makes unexpected demands on the knowledge, patience, and practical wisdom of the advisor. His counterpart and co-workers speak a different language and have different customs and preferences — external differences which can be easily observed and described. Their very obviousness, however, often obscures more subtle differences in patterns of thought and modes of action, and in concepts about the world and experience, which affect the interaction of the advisor and his counterpart.[2]

Assigning the Right Person or the Right Team.

Selecting the right individual to become an advisor is not a simple paperwork assignment process, and involves far more than his having rank and military knowledge. In the bureaucratic world, how-ever, such selection criteria may not be addressed or even understood, and advisors are often chosen for the wrong reasons. In addition, it may be more appropriate to assign an advisory team rather than a single individual, especially if the foreign official heads an agency or ministry whose work has a significant impact on the country's security or economy. Additionally, a position which is not advertised or regarded as an advisory slot may turn into just that if the American officer's personality is appropriate, or as work conditions evolve. At senior levels, position descriptions are never static, and a good advisor must be flexible as changes in his assignment occur.

Not every American officer is suited to be a good advisor for a foreign official. More than any other position in the military structure, the role implies a relationship between two individuals, and that relationship depends more on personality, psychology, and intangible factors than it does on an officer's personnel record or his technical expertise. While cultural and political knowledge can be gained through study and observation, the advisor must have the personality, patience, savvy, background, and interests which allow him to be open to such study, and open to the foreign environment in which he will find himself. The advisor should be comfortable with ambiguity, and willing to act based solely on higher intent, purpose, and policy objectives rather than a hard and fast list of instructions. He may be part of an advisory team, or he may be a solitary figure who acts without the immediate support or company of any other U.S. military or interagency colleagues. In either case, he must be able to adjust to this environment, absorb a vast amount of new information, and then act confidently, possibly without being able to consult his colleagues in advance.

Rank, Gender, and Age.

A young male captain or major may be the best soldier in the world and a great teacher. A female of any high rank may be a paragon of military ability and experience. In foreign eyes, however, they face great initial obstacles, and have a serious disadvantage compared to an older male officer of colonel to general officer rank.

Many foreigners do not accept contemporary American views about rank, gender, age, or race. Insisting that they do so will hinder or doom the advisory mission. It took the United States hundreds of years to reach today's stage in political and social sophistication, and it is counterproductive and illogical to insist that foreign cultures and foreign histories evolve the same way that America has.

The United States has made great strides in ensuring that gender, age, and racial considerations are not used to bar qualified applicants from employment or assignments. In the government and military services, men and women work side by side. Cabinet level and command positions in the military are routinely filled by women, and both law and custom now enshrine the principle that men and women are equal in every legal respect. This is not the case in many other countries, however, where gender and age are important consid-erations in selection for assignments, and where they are essential considerations in assessing someone's profes-sional merit. In a traditional Muslim country, for example, the advice of a young female officer would not have the importance of a male's advice, no matter what her experience or credentials were. And the words of a young male officer would not be considered nearly as valuable as those of an older man of higher rank. Ethnic background, skin color, and religious faith also play a role, based on local society and tradition. The result may translate into what Americans consider prejudice and discrimination. A good advisor will set a personal example of fairness, but cannot impose his standards on his foreign counterparts.

In traditional Muslim societies, a senior male foreign government official might find it unacceptable to be advised by a foreign female advisor. He might tolerate it on the surface, but would be unlikely in the initial stage to pay serious attention to her advice and might not be comfortable in her presence. The female advisor would find it difficult to accompany the official to many events, and being alone with him would be improper culturally. No matter how moral, professional, and correct she might be, an American female officer assigned such duties would have to overcome certain negative assumptions in foreign eyes. The female advisor may be able to overcome these cultural inhibitions against her success by force of personality and professional competence, but it will be a difficult uphill battle, consuming inordinate time and energy and possibly detracting from the advisory mission.

A lower ranking male or a female officer's expertise can break down these culturally inhibiting barriers over time, but it will also require an open attitude on the part of the foreign official. Possible techniques for success are to partner a junior officer or a female with a higher ranking advisor for the initial stage until their advisory chemistry clicks with the foreign official, or to incorporate them into a larger team.

Rank is real, whether earned or bestowed as a gift. Rows of medals carry weight in foreign eyes, and until proven otherwise, ribbons, medals, and insignia connote gravitas, intelligence, experience, entree, and authority. While it is not necessary to display these awards routinely, their ownership will be noted and judged. In traditional societies, they are signs of high rank, and an advisor of high rank is (initially, at least) much more acceptable to a foreign official and much more likely to command the official's attention and esteem. Rank introduced by insignia must also be reinforced in other ways, with the senior U.S. official in-country reminding the foreign official from time to time that the American advisor has his full confidence and that he relies on the advisor's counsel himself. This ongoing process of enhancing the advisor's legitimacy is important for all three parties, the senior American commander, the advisor, and the foreign official, since it confirms that the flow of information, decisions, and advice are valid and trustworthy.

IV. THE ADVISOR'S TOOLS FOR SUCCESS

Successful counsel is based heavily on both personal mindset and professional ability. The advisor must be ready to play the roles of both teacher and student, be open to an unfamiliar cultural environment, have evident interest and respect for unusual people and places, and be willing to subject his own comfort, preferences, and timing to those of a foreigner.

A good advisor will adjust to foreign culture and habits in order to enable his message and guidance to be presented effectively. He must be intellectually curious, and also be able to keep silent and just listen. It is also essential that an advisor have the professional and personal qualifications to perform his duties. However engaging his personality though, technical expertise in his field is an absolute requirement.

Professional, Academic, and Life Experience.

Being qualified does not just mean that the proposed advisor has attended a series of training courses, but touches on his personality, his social skills, his real world experience, his language fluency (or his dedication to learning the local language), and his professional credentials. The advisor's background and skills will be quickly judged by his foreign counterpart, and a senior foreign official is often highly trained and experienced in his own right. The official may also have high professional standing in his country and abroad.

The U.S. military system, on the other hand, does not normally generate national level expertise in any sector of study. If an individual had advanced university degrees in the energy field, for example, and had years of experience at progressively higher jobs in the U.S. energy sector, he would almost certainly not be an Army officer available to be assigned as an advisor to the local Minister of Energy in a foreign country. The real expert in a technological or other field is more likely to be a civilian contractor attached to the advisory team rather than the military officer, and collegiality and collaboration will be vital for success.

There are other criteria for success in the advisory mission. Does the advisor measure up to the local official enough in other ways to make his advice useful and acceptable?

In a foreign country which has gone through a lengthy period of war and political violence, anyone who has attained a senior position has undoubtedly seen many of his friends and relatives killed, has killed people himself, has led men into battle, and has possibly made life and death decisions repeatedly. Does the advisor's background or age give him credibility in the official's eyes? This is not just a question of what university degrees he possesses, but refers to an assessment the foreign official will make based on his own life experience.

If the advisor does not measure up in one aspect, he must recognize and acknowledge his limitations and give advice in that context. Some of this falls into the area of "how he advises" rather than "what he advises." The advisor must play to his strengths when opportunities arise and conditions permit, and look for ways that demonstrate his particular expertise and talents.

*****

It is difficult to know by what standards a foreign leader will judge an American. In an introductory conversation with a major and much feared Pashtun warlord in Afghanistan, an American diplomat began by listing the war zones and hardship assignments he had had, tying his life abroad to what hostilities were taking place at the time. But the warlord was oblivious to other countries' conflicts. Then the diplomat noted that over the course of his life he had been held by security officials in the United States and two foreign countries, eventually spending well over a year in prison abroad.

The warlord's single question was about the incident in America, and when told it involved a death, said simply "then I can talk to you."

*****

It is possible that a foreign official will have an advanced degree, significant experience in administration or another field, fluency in English, a second citizenship from a western country in addition to his birth country, and extensive professional and social ties to the United States and the greater world. Even if he does not have a university degree or speak English, the official might be fluent in several regional languages. Although he may not have attended a military academy, the official could be a veteran of decades of battle, fighting in the trenches and commanding units while the advisor was still a child. Even without a college degree in business or administration, the official could be a tribal or regional leader accustomed to administering vast areas of land, significant budgets, and large numbers of people. He might sit on the floor, wear a turban and flowing robes, and eat with his fingers, but his position of power is prima facie evidence that he has noteworthy experience, as well as social and political clout. In addition, the military advisor is highly unlikely to be the first American he has met, and he may already have extensive contacts with American and other foreign VIPs involved with his country.

At the most basic level, whatever the senior foreign official's exotic clothing or lack of Western polish, he has survived to exercise power when people with more exalted academic credentials, higher rank, and more important lineage have ended up dead or in prison. Understanding how this happened and analyzing the official's history can be an invaluable lesson for the American advisor in his efforts to develop a relationship and package his advice for success.

*****

Do not confuse paper with qualifications. Many American officials have "I love me" walls covered with framed academic degrees, innumerable commendations, and photos of themselves standing with VIPs. The wealthy and the educated have personal libraries and collections of antiques and art. But then there has not been a conflict on American soil since the Civil War. In Afghanistan, for example, the period beginning with the coup in 1973 and continuing through the Taliban era was one of house arrests, bombings, and armed attacks on government buildings and private homes. Photographs, art work, books, and documents were hastily abandoned as their owners fled to escape imprisonment or bombs. Confiscation, looting, and war damage took an immense toll on personal property, and there was a massive destruction or dispersal of family mementoes and cultural and historic items.

In politically unstable countries, the display of degrees or commendations issued by one regime can mean a jail sentence or execution under its successor. Shrewd officials are survivors, and more likely to keep such personal items safely out of sight.

*****

The advisor must show that he has qualifications that complement the official's skill set, and that he can add value to the official's performance and provide useful advice and assistance. If he cannot show he is of value, he will be ignored, relegated to the role of foreign staff aide, or at best be only a liaison between the official's office and the local U.S. military bureaucracy. How he does this will differ with time and location, but it is a challenge that he must analyze and meet in order to accomplish his mission.

The Advisor's Personality.

Providing counsel is not a 9 to 5 position, just as being a Cabinet member or a Governor is not a 40-hour-a-week job. Advisors are on call 24/7, and a good advisor will be an accepted and expected presence at any and all times. The advisor who has to make an appointment through a secretary and wait hours or days to see his counterpart official may already have failed in his job.

*****

A recent American Political Advisor to a non-U.S. NATO PRT Commander, for example, shared a tent with the Commander, ate breakfast with him every day, accompanied him to a variety of external meetings throughout the day, participated at all evening staff meetings for the PRT's leadership, often joined the Commander for dinner, and sometimes ended with an informal conversation at night. It was the informal contact at meals or in the late evenings, when both could speak frankly, that the best opportunities came to discuss modes of action or offer advice, not at the official meetings.

*****

Personal Flexibility.

There is a difference between the activities of a Governor or a Cabinet Minister and those of a PRT Commander. The two former have provinces or the whole country as their domains, while the latter's life is circumscribed by the perimeter of the base and a limited area of operations. The life styles of top-level officials make it less likely that advisors will have or even want to have constant access. The Governor and Minister, after all, will have family, social, and political worlds, as well as future agendas which are closed to the advisor. However, the advisor must be willing and able to relegate his own schedule and preferences to those of the senior official.

For most senior officials, there is no demarcation line between work and down-time. Whether the official gets up before dawn to pray and eat breakfast, or does his best thinking and makes decisions at midnight with a bottle of whisky, the advisor should be known to be available. If the Governor or Minister prefers to sit on the floor, thumb his prayer beads, and listen to flute and drum music, the advisor should be adept at taking his boots off and resting cross-legged for a few hours at a time. In many parts of the Muslim world, privacy is not a value or even much of a concept, and the American advisor should be willing to adapt to

27

discussions held in loud social settings, or to talking with the official while 10 or 20 or even 50 others are sitting in the room and listening silently. The locations may range from quiet, private meetings to crowded public affairs where the proceedings are all captured by the local TV cameras, and the advisor will need to adjust to the social venue and show himself to be comfortable in it.

Knowing the Local Culture.

The American advisor should seek local guidance on cultural and social custom and etiquette, watch others around him, and ask questions about proper norms of behavior from local sources. He cannot assume that what goes for his home region in America is appropriate in Iraq, Yemen, Israel or Pakistan. No "one size fits all" book on etiquette and culture encompasses the wide variety of the Islamic world. Every country has its own set of "do's and don'ts," and various practices or prohibitions may even change from town to town. Differences between foreign and American etiquette are endless, and ignorance of local customs will harm the advisor's effectiveness. No one can possibly know everything about a foreign culture — or even his own culture — but some basic humility, an open mind, intellectual curiosity, and the ability to laugh at himself will carry the advisor a very long way. He must be aware of what is merely permissible, what is recommended, and what is prohibited in the local environment, because if local norms are not respected, the advisor's best efforts to present ideas and influence foreign officials will be frustrated or even counterproductive.

The learning process can be a lengthy one, and everyone makes mistakes along the road, but the more an advisor is versed and feels comfortable in the foreign social setting, the more effective his presentation of advice will be. Some social settings may be difficult for the advisor, but he will adapt quickly if he wants to be successful. After all, decisionmaking is a continuous process, and final decisions are often made far from the office setting.

Even informal social settings can be a minefield for the unwary, and what is normal and ordinary in the United States might be considered rude, embarrassing, and very detrimental to the advisor's mission. For example, concepts of personal space are different in many Muslim countries, and the American may find himself far too close physically to other men to be comfortable, with guests leaning against him while everyone is eating or simply sitting down to talk. It is not unusual for Muslim men to walk hand in hand, or to hold hands far longer than a quick American handshake would allow. In the United States, men and women will shake hands or possibly even kiss cheeks on first meeting, an act that would be inconceivable by conservative Islamic norms. For example, blowing one's nose in public is regarded as repulsive in Iran and Afghanistan, as much a turn-off as picking one's nose in public would be in the United States. Asking personal questions about an official's wife or daughter (or describing one's own) might be absolutely routine and acceptable in a western meeting, but would be considered insulting in a conservative Muslim setting. And in these settings, the American officer who tries to show a foreign counterpart personal photos of female relatives in order to display a common bond of "family" would immediately lose face in conservative Muslim eyes.

A foreign official in Afghanistan may simply take one's hand and clasp it for long periods during a conversation, or want to walk arm in arm, which can cause angst and discomfort for many American men, especially if the media is filming the event and it is likely to appear in the American press. Removing boots and shoes is absolutely necessary in many Middle East and South Asian settings, especially in private homes. Keeping them on per U.S. military regulations marks the offender as uncouth. Wearing body armor or carrying a weapon into homes and office settings shows clearly that the American does not trust his hosts and will cast an unwelcome pall over any conversation, or alternatively, imply that the American is afraid of his surroundings. The American habit of chewing tobacco and spitting the remnants into a water bottle is considered disgusting in most cultures, but on the other hand, in Yemen men spend hours every day chewing a narcotic leaf called "qat," spitting green liquid residue directly into convenient bowls. Participating in these lengthy and drowsy sessions is often the only way to accomplish one's work.

Orders of precedence are essential to understand. In Afghanistan and Iran, for example, a host will always gesture for a guest to precede him through a door. This is acceptable and expected in an informal setting, for example at the official's home. In the office, however, or at any official meeting or inspection where walking together in public is in order, the advisor's going first would be considered a sign of boorish behavior and lack of respect for the foreign official.

The protocol of eating is profoundly important in many places, and ignoring it can sink a mission. Taking refreshments like coffee and tea, or eating local food are essential for the advisor to establish a relationship with the official or any host. Foreigners are watched carefully and judged by their willingness to partake in proffered hospitality, and in some areas they might actually be at risk until they have shown they are friendly by accepting refreshment (e.g., in the Pashtun tribal belt). Refusing food and drink will chill the atmosphere and put up obstacles to an advisor's relationship with any official. Pulling out an MRE after refusing local food is an extreme insult.

*****

On a trip in a remote part of Afghanistan's Ghor Province, a PRT Commander and his Political Advisor stopped at a small road side tea house to talk to the villagers gathered there. The Commander, who really did not want to drink anything, politely turned down the offered tea. Turning to the local villagers, the tea house owner said in Dari, "These foreigners think what we eat and drink is dirty." If the POLAD had not understood the comment and quietly told the Commander to accept the tea, the atmosphere would have turned very cold very quickly.

*****

Sometimes hospitality can be carried to extremes. At a Pashtun banquet in northern Pakistan when an American diplomat was guest of honor of a large group of clergy at a refugee camp, a whole roast sheep was carried in on a tray. The bearded host reached his hand under the sheep's tail and pulled out a large wad of semi raw fat, holding it up to the American official's mouth and saying, "Eat. It's the best part." Swallowing the suet directly from his host's hand with a nod of thanks was the only way to continue the momentum of the conversation.

*****

Expecting every Muslim to follow every rule expressed in the *Quran* is like expecting every Christian to obey every stricture laid down in the Bible. It is not going to happen in this world. For example, despite Islamic prohibitions, some people in Muslim countries — including high officials — drink alcohol. And no culture has ever managed to completely outlaw sexual misadventures. If alcohol flows too freely or prostitutes are brought in after dinner, the American advisor may wish to excuse himself, but he must do so in a way that does not detract from the official's standing in front of other people or denigrate the proffered hospitality. Including the American in such entertainment can be a sign that he has been accepted as a trusted advisor, but it can also be a sign that the official wants to entangle him in his personal corruption. There is no hard and fast rule for telling the difference, and the advisor must make on-the-spot decisions based on his own knowledge of local norms and his own perception of what is right.

Advisors are human, and there will be a line beyond which one cannot go, foods one cannot eat, gifts that one cannot accept, and behavior that one cannot tolerate. Personal principles and standards of integrity should not be sacrificed, and it is always acceptable to just say "no," as long as it is done politely, firmly, and with no hint of condemnation. A simple explanation of "why" — an explanation that should never become a self-righteous sermon — is perfectly acceptable in most cases.

Remember that a foreign advisor is always under observation, from servants, other guests, and the eyes of scores of nameless security guards, drivers, other staff, and even the beggars sitting outside along the road (who may be reporting his activities to the local security service). His reputation and his actions will be discussed and analyzed in circles of whose existence he is not even aware. He will be tested repeatedly to gauge his reactions and standards, and his character and professionalism judged accordingly. People he has never met will judge him from afar, and be ready to deal with him or refuse him access based on word on the street about his behavior. In some ways the new advisor is fortunate, because if he had been born in the country where he is assigned, his father's and grandfather's reputations would also have been factored into this equation.

It is not possible to describe the cultural and etiquette niceties in all parts of the Islamic world in a single document. As simple an act as drinking tea can have endless variations, sometimes within the immediate vicinity. Is it herbal tea from an unfamiliar plant, mint tea, red cinnamon tea, yellow cardamom tea, black tea, or green tea? Is there a tea bag, or are there fresh leaves floating in the water? Is it served in a porcelain cup, a bowl, or a glass? Does it come to the guest already (and heavily) presweetened, or mixed with milk? Is it presented with an elaborate service of china and silver, from a plastic thermos, from a brass samovar, or straight from the fire in a blackened and battered tea kettle? Is the sweetener a piece of wrapped candy, a sugar cube, rock sugar on a swizzle stick, or granulated sugar? Is there a spoon to mix the sugar, or is the guest expected to hold a sugar cube in his mouth and let the tea pass through the cube as he sips? How does one indicate that he does not want a refill? Placing a spoon across the tea glass? Turning the glass over? Lifting the eyebrows to indicate "no, thanks"? Experience is the best teacher for the advisor—and simply watching what others around him are doing and being flexible and adaptable are the only realistic guides to understanding and appreciating the local culture.

What is the bottom line? Social customs and behavior differ from one place to another, and the advisor will have to put this into perspective and practice some degree of flexibility. A successful advisor will study and ask about local social norms, and adjust in an appropriate way to the setting while maintaining his personal principles and standards. If he cannot adapt physically and psychologically to the foreign environment, it is likely that his advice and expertise will also not be adaptable to the foreign reality.

Knowing American Culture and History.

Advisors serve as a quick reference for any and all questions that foreign officials have about the United States, ranging from etiquette points to serious discussions about American history, religion, politics, and policy. An advisor who cannot intervene in a meeting to correct misconceptions, or who cannot explain the U.S. political system, the basics of democracy, the concept and practice of rule of law, the history of race relations in American society, the meaning of the President's latest speech shown that morning on local television, general U.S. policy towards the host country, and myriad other questions will quickly lose credibility. And the questions may be tough, coming from unexpected sources. A senior official might be polite and sophisticated, but the local high school students or congregants at a local mosque that the advisor is visiting with his foreign colleagues may be blunt and merciless when they ask an American advisor "Why the American Army has invaded their country" or "Why does the United States persecute Muslims"? Remember that an advisor is more than a technical assistant: he may be the only representative in many settings of America writ large, and can win friends or make enemies for the United States based on his knowledge of his own country.

Knowing the Terrain.

Advice is useless if given in a vacuum. In theory, the advisor must know everything possible about the history, society, culture, economy, and politics of the country to which he is assigned if his advice is to have any connection to the reality of the foreign official's world. In fact, however, the advisor will rarely have had the luxury of years of study about the country, and so the process of knowing in itself becomes important. He should strive to learn as much as he can, and show interest, enthusiasm, and commitment to the learning process, because knowledge of the local human terrain will determine the nature of his advice, the way it is presented, and the likelihood that it will be received and implemented. It will impact directly on the relationship between the advisor and the foreign official, and make all the difference between success and failure in his mission.

This knowledge has no substitute, and it can only be acquired by watching, listening, and studying over time. However, a senior official has the right to assume from the first meeting that his advisor has at least a general background in the country's history and politics, and that the advisor's questions are based on existing knowledge of the region and the country. Being totally ignorant is an insult to the foreign official and a waste of his time. More importantly, the official may logically conclude that the ignorance of the advisor on human terrain issues is a reflection of ignorance of his purported speciality.

*****

An Afghan VIP recently noted that he refused to deal with anyone from International Security Assistance Force (ISAF) Headquarters in Kabul because all too often the ISAF representatives were unprepared for the meetings and wasted his time. He expressed his vexation by saying "They don't know anything about Afghanistan. They were even asking me the names of our former Presidents."

*****

On another occasion, a very senior American official visiting Afghanistan had been fully briefed about the new Afghan Parliament and had been provided extensive background material well in advance of his meeting with the Parliamentary leadership. However, instead of discussing policy issues with national-level leaders, he spent the meeting asking very basic questions about the numbers of members, the mechanics of the election process, etc., indicating to the senior Afghan officials present that he knew very little about the country or its government, and missing the opportunity for a political discussion at the strategic level.

*****

The advisor must understand American policy, and know the limits of what he can and cannot say or do. He cannot exceed the parameters established by his commander or the Ambassador. Exceeding his authority may leave the advisor in a position where his credibility disappears, and thus he will no longer be able to perform his duties.

The Hypocrisy Factor.

The advisor must remember that his foreign audience may see him differently than he views himself, and will react to his advice accordingly. If the American government or the local command and/or embassy disregard international norms of behavior or human rights, for example, the advisor's best advice to a foreign official may be met with disdain. The advisor will be judged by his audience as the representative of a larger power, and seen in the light of that power's own actions.

Sometimes the physical circumstances of the advisor's presentation may negate his message as well, causing an unwelcome reaction in his listeners, especially if they become embarrassed or insulted.

*****

An American Task Force Commander in Afghanistan made an unannounced visit to a remote district of Herat Province, accompanied by an Afghan General and several civilian visitors as well. They traveled in a large convoy of more than 20 vehicles filled with well-armed American and Afghan soldiers, about 100 in all as a display meant to cow the district officials. The district administrator was summoned to appear before the colonel and his entourage, and subjected to a long public speech by the American officer about the necessity of collecting all the weapons held by the district residents. The Afghan administrator waited until the colonel was finished, and then said simply:"There are more than 200 villages in this district, and every house has a weapon. We have almost no police enforcement here. If you promise me that every time a village family has a problem you will come immediately from the capital to solve it, I will happily collect all the weapons. But Colonel, come unarmed and not with all these soldiers. You shouldn't tell us to get rid of all our weapons unless you are brave enough to come alone and unarmed to talk about it."

*****

Despite their good intentions, many foreigners are perceived as hypocrites by Muslim audiences, and their message met with annoyance or even anger because of the manner it is presented. A highly paid, expensively dressed American who arrives in a costly armored vehicle and is accompanied by well-armed security guards will not win votes of confidence or brotherhood from villagers who make a pittance, live in mud houses, and are overwhelmed by the daily grind of sheer physical survival. The very concept of the non-Muslim American trying to lecture such village crowds about proper Islamic teachings or moral behavior is ironic, but unfortunately a common occurrence. The normal reaction is indignation, politely disguised by the listeners, but sometimes the response can be far stronger.

*****

In a speech before a Pashtun audience, a senior American official in Afghanistan decided to lecture them about the error of their ways in continuing to raise opium poppies. He pointed his finger at the crowd and told them harshly that they should be ashamed of their behavior. Instead of winning the crowd to his point of view, the reaction was one of anger and extreme resentment, rising all the way to the top level of the Afghan government and resulting in very negative publicity. In the Afghan culture, pointing fingers and using the word "shame" are considered as personal insults.

*****

V. THE LANGUAGE PROBLEM

The ideal advisor should be fluent in the local language, but this ideal is rarely met. Professional relationships, accuracy, and security will all be affected by the advisor's inability to speak the language. Most advisors use interpreters, making it difficult to establish a truly effective relationship with the senior local official they are advising. The proper use of interpreters is often difficult in itself. Even if everyone speaks English, the advisor must be sensitive to differences in understanding which are caused by differences in background and life experience. None of this is impossible, but language is a complicating factor in relationships and requires close attention.

The history of language training for American diplomats and military assigned to post-war Iraq and Afghanistan has been problematic. The more senior the American advisor, the less likely it is that he will have had time for intensive language study or been able to absorb what he was taught. Even the junior officer who studies Arabic, Dari, or Pashtu in the United States may find that he has little opportunity to immerse himself in the language within the host country because his contact with native speakers may be very limited. The present security practice of restricting personal movement outside American compounds means that day-to-day dealings with the local populace are often very limited, and thus the American officer may not make much language progress while actually assigned to the country. In many cases, language fluency actually decreases once the officer arrives at his post.

If the foreign official does not speak fluent English, it is far more likely that the advisor will communicate (1) through an interpreter, (2) through a simplified version of English which appears comprehensible to the official, or (3) through a third language which the advisor and the foreign official share. All of these have pros and cons, and directly affect the advisor's effectiveness.

Use of Interpreters.

The perfect interpreter is impossible to find, but the advisor must cope nonetheless. Who is an ideal interpreter? It would be someone who can accurately and quickly translate nuanced meaning, be thoroughly versed in both countries' history, literature, culture, and politics, as well as in the technical subjects under discussion, and yet not allow his personality to shade the interpretation. This paragon does not exist, and if he did, the advisor would not be able to afford him.

In the real world, the interpreter is more likely a local citizen who left his country decades in the past and has only returned on a contract, or someone whose parents are from the country in question and who learned the language from his family while growing up in America, or a local citizen who studied English in school. None of these is likely to be a formally trained interpreter, and, at best, the American advisor will be provided translation which will only be approximately correct. Facts, figures, and details will often be mistranslated, and nuances of meaning may be totally lost.

If the interpreter is from a different religious or ethnic group than the official, there may be mistrust and bias on both sides. If the interpreter is seen as having abandoned his native country for a better life in America, there may be resentment against him from officials who stayed and fought through the hard times in the country's history. At worst, the interpreter will have such heavy emotional baggage, prejudice, or personal political motivation that conversations will be twisted in a way not intended by either advisor or official, leading to distrust and mission failure. All of this adds immeasurably to the advisor's burden.

Dealing with interpreters is a skill which a surprisingly large number of senior officials and advisors completely lack, but not having this skill is like not knowing how to fire your weapon. Common mistakes by American officers are to subject the interpreter to long, rambling philosophical perorations which no one — sometimes even other Americans — could easily understand; to assume that the interpreter can memorize long paragraphs of convoluted speech; to assume that the interpreter can understand obscure metaphors, regional American dialect, professional jargon, slang, and acronyms; and to assume that the interpreter actually intends to translate everything rather than simply giving a synopsis of the conversation.

The only way to avoid these pitfalls is to speak slowly, clearly, and succinctly, to rehearse key points in advance with the interpreter, and to check and recheck the interpreter's accuracy with figures and other data. Even then, however, no translation will be completely correct, and inaccuracies and bias on the interpreter's part may color the advisor's intended statements.

The advisor can improve his message by avoiding military jargon and abbreviations. "Military-speak" can be so heavily laden with acronyms and special vocabulary that it is even incomprehensible to American civilians. Metaphors, similes, and humor are difficult to translate well into other cultures. If the advisor has studied a foreign language, he will remember how difficult it is to articulate concepts and specifics. This simple consideration is a crucial lesson in understanding the burden placed on an interpreter, and the necessity of helping prepare him to accomplish his job.

*****

Any comment about a Muslim female's physical attributes can be a precept for disaster. Her male relatives might consider it an insult to the family honor.

*****

Telling a Turk or an Iranian that he is "working like a dog" or is "as stubborn as a donkey" can be fighting words, because comparisons to animals are considered insults.

*****

Asking an interpreter to repeat back what you have said or plan to say improves the chances of accuracy. The advisor should avoid analogies, and recognize that an interpreter may drop a point, or guess at it, if he has not fully understood the concept. Most of all, the advisor should not surprise the interpreter with unusual vocabulary or new subjects of discourse. Arcane references to American history will be lost on both the interpreter and the audience, and university level lectures on political development or philosophy should be left in the university, not addressed to tribal leaders.

Privately reviewing what you plan to say with the interpreter before a meeting allows him to understand the new vocabulary and concepts before he has to explain them to the senior official. An interpreter who may know every word necessary to discuss al-Qaeda or taking apart an M-4 may not have any vocabulary at all in other fields the advisor wants to discuss. The interpreter's fluency in one subject should not be confused with vocabulary expertise or familiarity with other topics.

An interpreter is always pulled between two worlds, and it may place him in personal danger. If there is an active opposition to the presence of U.S. forces in the country, an interpreter's life and his family's security can be at stake. Interpreters might be regarded as traitors by their neighbors or opposition groups, and their activities will be monitored. They may be susceptible to threats if they do not pass on information to opposition groups or insurgents, or to death if the opposition has declared that collaboration with U.S. forces is a crime. Unlike the advisor, whose family is safely out of reach in the United States, the interpreter must take his extended family's security and future into constant consideration. In Iraq, for example, there is a clear security threat to interpreters because they enable U.S. military forces to function with local leaders. The interpreters become primary targets.

By extension, the advisor's behavior and activities will also affect his interpreter's personal and family security. In one case in Herat, Afghanistan, for example, an Afghan guard force chief previously employed at the PRT was killed along with his entire family when gunmen broke into their residence. Coincidence or political retribution? In another case, an interpreter in Kabul was asked to stay late one evening. He agreed, but asked that he be allowed to sleep at the base that night, because "going home so late in the evening will make my neighbors think I have a different job than the story I told them." His neighborhood was conservative and anti-western, and gossip about his work with the Americans would have posed a danger to his family.

It is not only political sensitivity that makes going home late difficult. In Kabul, Afghan employees who had to stay at work far into the night had to face the dangers of road blocks and robbers if they traveled home on the empty, dark streets. Even if there was good security, the lack of street lighting, proper sidewalks, and paved roads made night-time travel physically difficult.

In recognition of the security threat to military interpreters, programs are now in place to allow them to obtain special immigration visas to the United States. An advisor should learn about these programs from the Embassy consular section and be willing to give honest answers to an interpreter when he asks about the possibility of leaving his country.

Using "Basic" English.

Problems are also associated with reliance on the foreign official's knowledge of English. Unless the official is very fluent, the advisor may be misunderstood even while both assume they understand each other perfectly. Pigeon English and mime are fine in a bar or restaurant; they do not work well when the subjects are politics, strategy, and security issues.

Even when both parties speak English well, differences exist between American usage and British/Australian/other usage which can lead to misunderstandings. These differences can be the more treacherous because they are totally unexpected, and each side of the discussion assumes that the other understands him perfectly.

The same can be true of Arabic from country to country, of Turkish, Persian, and so on. Because dialects change from region to region, what one assumes is mutual understanding can instead be mutual incomprehension.

*****

At the entrance of the teachers' room for the English Language Department at Haceteppe University in Ankara, Turkey, a box was once placed to collect the blackboard erasers used by the language instructors returning from classes. The department's British secretary wrote a very clear instruction sign for the British, American and Turkish teachers--all of whom shared the English language, which had a very different meaning for the British/Turks than it did for the Americans. The sign read, "Teachers, please put your used rubbers in this box."

*****

At a dinner in the Iranian Province of Azerbaijan, an American Peace Corps volunteer who spoke the Turkish of neighboring Turkey tried to thank his hostess and turn down offers of another full plate by saying that it was "too much" and he had already eaten "too much." He emphasized the Turkish word for "too much" by pointing at his dish. The host family reacted with stunned silence, and only after an English-speaking participant asked what the volunteer really meant, did the group dissolve into laughter. The word for "too much" in Ankara's Turkish meant "mouse shit" in the local dialect. The American guest had been telling his hostess that there were feces on his plate.

*****

Using a Third Language.

Using a language which the advisor and the official share, but which is not the mother language of either one, can also compound the possibilities for error and misunderstandings. An added dimension is that it may be a language which has unwelcome political overtones. Languages are tools of communication, but they also carry historic and cultural connotations of which the advisor must be aware. For the American who learned a language during an idyllic stay abroad as a student, a second language may bring memories of only good times and youthful adventure. For a foreign official or others who hear the same sounds, that language may be an unpleasant subconscious reminder of death and injury to family and friends.

*****

Hearing Americans speak Russian with Afghan officials can be an unpleasant subconscious reminder to Afghans of the Soviet invasion and occupation of Afghanistan. Was Russian the language heard by the official as a child when orders were being given to arrest his father? Even if the official was once on the side of the Soviets, others in his entourage may have served painful times in prison being mistreated by Russian-speaking guards and interrogators.

*****

Sometimes the language spoken inside the house is not the official language of the country. Using one or the other can build imperceptible walls between people, especially if the official language implies social or political dominance by another ethnic group. An American once assigned to Iran realized that speaking Farsi with ethnic Turks from the

Iranian province of Azerbaijan placed social barriers between them, just as his speaking Turkish with Kurdish friends in Turkey did. Both the Turks of western Iran and the Kurds of Turkey felt discrimination and pressure as members of minority groups, and part of the ongoing ethnic tension involved the choice of which language to use.

*****

Understanding What Is Heard and What Is Said: When the Advisor's Terms of Reference Are Not Those of the Foreign Official.

Understanding the differences in connotation of words and differences in concepts is essential for the advisor if he is to communicate effectively.

> Even though a word may be found to translate a concept from one cultural pattern to another, there is no assurance that an accurate and viable concept has been chosen in the second pattern that is equivalent to the original one. When two cultures are not parallel in their focal points, misunderstandings can occur and inaccuracies can be perpetrated by the application of familiar concepts in a foreign environment. Americans and other Westerners have taken political and social concepts such as nationalism, militarism, and the democratic system of elections, which are native to Western countries, and have attempted to apply them to underdeveloped countries where they have different meanings.[3]

Originally written about the work of advisors in Vietnam in the 1960s, this is true as well in today's Afghanistan, Iraq, and Kosovo. The word "crime," for example, is easily translated into Dari, but the average Afghan has a very different concept of what constitutes crime than an American.

In the United States, there is no legal problem (or even any legal implication) in converting from one religious faith to another, while in Afghanistan, and the larger Muslim world, conversion from Islam to another religion is considered a serious crime. When national identity, family identity, and Islam are inextricably connected, apostasy is equivalent to treason and betrayal of one's kinfolk.

In the United States, killing one's wife, sister, or daughter for having an extra-marital relationship would be a crime, but *not* doing so in some parts of the world shows one as weak and dishonorable, with no regard for family, clan, or tribal honor codes. Taking justice into one's own hands and killing someone who had insulted or badly offended you would be a crime in America, but in other places might be considered natural and even necessary. Not to retaliate might show you as weak and feckless, and thus place you and your family in greater danger.

Even perceptions of historic events are affected by geography. In the west, the names "Attila" and "Genghis" might conjure images of Attila the Hun and Genghis Khan, regarded as blood thirsty conquerors who ravaged vast areas and almost brought an end to western civilization. In Turkey and other Asian countries, they are often seen as national heroes. In the west, the word "crusade" has a positive connotation, while in the Muslim world it is a reminder of European invasion and the attempted destruction of Islamic civilization by western armies. By the same token, a devout Muslim sees a religious and positive connotation in the word "jihad," while an American thinks of suicide bombers and terrorism when he hears it.

The list of conflicting concepts goes on and on. "Rule of law," "democracy," "extending the reach of the central government," "Hamas," "football," "the Taliban," "honor," "tomorrow"--all of these are easy to translate or may even sound the same in other languages, but the very words used for these and many more concepts may have radically different connotations for the American advisor and the senior official with whom he is talking. Is football a game where the players use heavy padding and throw the ball, or one where they wear shorts and kick the ball? Is "Hamas" a terrorist organization, or a charitable institution which brings help to needy communities? Is "tomorrow" what occurs after midnight, or a hazy, indeterminate time in a possible future? Are the Taliban the insurgents so demonized in American political rhetoric and the U.S. media, or a movement which brought stability to an Afghanistan reeling from civil war. Does "extending the reach of the central government" mean to bring much needed services and stability to remote areas, or is it just a way to send strangers from the capital city to the provinces so that rural areas can be looted and abused more easily?

This does not mean that communication is impossible, or forever part of the Tower of Babel. What it does mean is that communication is not always easy, and the advisor must take special care to ensure that he really understands what he hears, and that his own meaning is conveyed accurately when he speaks.

There are ways to minimize the difficulties and achieve the advisor's goals. Beginning to learn the local language — or at least the minimal expressions of courtesy and greeting — is an important first step. Self-study and help from interpreters can assist the advisor in this. Even learning one or two new words a day can lead to an extensive working vocabulary in a short time.

Non-verbal Communication.

Paying close attention to facial and body language and other forms of nonverbal communication is also important for the advisor, and allows him to gauge reaction before the words are translated. Over time, as the advisor and the senior official become familiar with one another, and as the advisor works to understand the language, gestures, and local customs, communication will become easier.

Signs, facial expressions, and physical gestures that Americans take for granted and routinely use while talking may have far different meanings in other cultures, and an advisor must be very careful to understand the signals he is sending. For examples, lifting the eyebrows signifies "no" in Turkey, and may not necessarily be accompanied by the spoken word, and the "thumbs up" gesture so commonly used by Americans to signify "good work" or " O.K." has a sexual connotation in some Muslim areas, and congratulating a local soldier by the thumbs-up gesture may cause the advisor unwanted speculation or ridicule from the group of young men who return the gesture with laughter. Ditto for holding the thumb and forefinger together in a circle to signal that something is, or tastes, good. In Turkey it was used as a signal for the sex act.

No one expects a foreigner to understand everything about a new culture immediately, but the advisor is in a public position and should ask his foreign colleagues to point out any obvious nonverbal mistakes. If he sees that laughter or embarrassed smiles break out when he makes a gesture, it is a sign that he should quietly ask someone if there was a problem.

VI. THE OFFICE AS BATTLE SPACE

The advisor must study his counterpart, learning his history and his cultural and social milieu. He must come to understand what affects the official's thought process and decisionmaking, and learn the local factors that determine the senior foreign official's ultimate success. While much basic information about a foreign official can be obtained from Google, news accounts on the internet, and intel sources prior to beginning an assignment, the best way for an advisor to understand his counterpart comes through physical proximity and observation over time.

The First Who in Who's Who.

Knowing as much as possible about his counterpart is imperative for the advisor. Learning the truth, however, is a subtle and time-consuming process. If the foreign official has come to public attention before, there will be miscellaneous information on Google about him. He may have an official biographical page to give to foreign visitors, and there is presumably information available through intelligence sources as well. Over time, the official will also share personal information about himself, but he will undoubtedly have a negative reaction if he feels that he is being interrogated about his private life.

The questions to be answered are legion. What is the official's history and lineage? His religion? His ethnic background? How did he get his senior position? Was he chosen by merit or based on political/ethnic/family patronage? To whom is he married, and what does his wife's family do? Is he personally close to the Head of State? Is he a relative? If so, by blood or by marriage?

Is he related to other members of the government, to Cabinet officials, to Parliamentarians, to leading security officials? Does he have ties through family, residence abroad, schooling, or business interests to other countries? What is his general reputation? While no single answer to any of these questions in and of itself will determine the official's receptivity to the American advisor, the answers will predispose him to certain paths of action.

Understanding the nature and structure of the senior official's office and agency is as important as knowing a battlefield before an engagement. The organization, the staffing, the place in the government structure, and the duties and responsibilities of the official and his colleagues are all essential knowledge for an advisor.

Knowing who is who, and who is related to whom, is vital. In less-developed countries, it is likely that many (or all) office positions are filled based on political, ethnic, regional, or family patronage. This is neither good nor bad, but simply a fact which reflects local social and political realities. It is generally not something within the advisor's purview to change, but he should understand these connections in order to make them useful for his own mission.

In the U.S. government, relatives rarely work in the same offices, and it would be highly improper for a supervisor to have a close family member in his chain of command. In a more traditional country, a minister or governor may have a close relative—a brother, nephew or brother-in-law—working in his immediate office, and this individual has access to the official in a way that no stranger ever could.

While Imam Khomeini ruled Iran, for example, his son Ahmad served the function of "gatekeeper" to his father, controlling entrée to the Supreme Leader.

Advice, recommendations, or information given informally to someone in this position will reach the senior official privately and allow him time to reflect before making a public decision. It is often far easier — and more acceptable culturally — to be frank with such an individual when it would not be possible to be so direct with a top official. A bad message will still get through, but in a way that saves face for everyone. In addition, it is possible that VIPs in the country are related through marriage, and that they have placed blood relatives in one another's offices to strengthen their political relationships and ease their communications with one another. The American advisor's words to one senior official will thus reach other senior officials as well.

There is a corollary to this placement. Relationships to high officials are not always apparent or disclosed. Even brothers might have different family names in some Muslim countries, making it difficult for an American to link counterparts to one another. For example, in Afghanistan, senior officials sometimes use their own younger brothers or nephews — people of rank themselves — to act as servants at social gatherings, in much the same way that medieval lords used their squires. Never assume that the silent young man who bows while offering you water to wash your hands is only a humble servant. He could be a governor-in-training and a trusted confidant of the senior official, and thus the American advisor's best bet for having unimpeded and immediate contact with the senior official.

Foreign Officials' Sources of Income.

It is not normally within the military advisor's scope of duties to try to transform the whole economic and financial basis of a country, or to reconstruct the bureaucracy or the retirement system. It is, however, in his interest to know the nature of the local system in order to tailor his advice and his expectations to reality. Knowing how local officials and bureaucrats are paid is essential to the advisor, because income sources directly affect decisionmaking.

In the underdeveloped regions of the Muslim world, the disparity between rich and poor may be severe, with both extremes reflected in the bureaucracy of the senior official's agency. The marble clad homes, gilt furniture, chandeliers, and fully-packed SUVs or luxury cars of the top staff will stand in stark contrast to the crowded adobe mud structures inhabited by low-ranking workers.

People require services from their government, and services — and the officials who provide them — require funding. If a country has no noteworthy natural resources to export for income (e.g., the way that Saudi Arabia has oil) and if the inhabitants do not routinely pay taxes (e.g., Afghanistan), the funding must be obtained somehow, and there is a certain efficiency in simply demanding that people who want services performed directly pay those who perform them.

Sources of national income at all levels may have little relationship to what the Budget Office has in its ledgers. Is the salary structure set by regulation, or is it based on fees for service, on the order of American waiters and waitresses who receive only a token salary from the restaurant owner and make their real income in tips from customers? Is taking a gift or bribe the normal state of affairs? How large can bribes be and still be acceptable, or is it full no-holds-barred in the bribery arena? Is there a well-understood and expected "payment for service" that satisfies both officials and the public — say 10 to 40 percent over and above the published fee — and on which government bureaucrats rely to supplement meager official salaries?

Is it really corruption for a low level worker, policeman, or soldier to ask for a few dollars as a gift when he would otherwise not have enough income to feed his family? Do workers in the agency have to pay off more senior officers in order to get a job? Is acquiring an office a one-time purchase, or a percentage of the official's salary every month to those higher up the chain? Does anyone in the hierarchy actually receive a living wage, or are they all expected to supplement their incomes by demanding additional money from people who need their service (e.g., contractors or supplicants) or from people who want to get promoted or get better assignments within the official's agency?

In much of the developing world, the western concept of "conflict of interest" is incomprehensible. Senior officials do not place their assets into a blind trust when they assume office. Rather, many assume office in order to get rich, and paying for office can be a normal procedure at all levels of the bureaucracy, just as enriching their families and friends through their office can be regarded as normal behavior.

It is highly unlikely that a senior foreign official is living on his salary alone, and the real sources of his income may predispose him to courses of action that may not be in the American advisor's interests. In a country (e.g., Afghanistan) that is corrupted by the narcotics trade, for example, senior security or civil officials may be taking in such large amounts of drug money that an American advisor will find it very difficult to realistically influence security policies. If the official's children study abroad thanks to foreign government scholarships, and his business interests are tied to contracts from other countries, it is also less likely that the American advisor's words will have much clout.

The system becomes somewhat more understandable when one realizes that many in the bribe-paying public often do not pay income tax to the government, paying unofficial fees (bribes?) instead when they actually require a government service. It also becomes more understandable when a government has no realistic retirement system. Since they know they cannot rely on receiving a pension once they retire, police, military, and civil service bureaucrats have to earn money for their retirements while they are actually working.

Local Perception of Government Service.

The advisor must understand where his ministry or government agency fits in the popular mind, and whether it has a popular constituency and support. While the local populace may fully understand the role and importance of a Police Commander, the work of the "Director of the Anti-Corruption Commission" may be unknown and/or completely disregarded by the man on the street.

In the United States there is an assumption that government officials, police and military are basically service-oriented, professional, educated and honest. Exceptions occur, of course, but the general view of the American public towards government is positive. This is not true in many other countries, and knowing how the public regards senior officials and/or their bureaucracies is important for the American advisor. Is there an overall feeling of respect and satisfaction, or do ordinary people think of the official and his staff as corrupt and inefficient? Is there popular resentment? Does the senior official have a history of war crimes, human rights abuse, theft, etc? Have the official and his staff been vetted for human rights violations by the appropriate organizations to allow them to receive security assistance and training in accordance with American regulations?

Expectations are important as well. What does the local populace expect of the official and his staff? Conducting surveys in Afghan villages in 2003, for example, the U.S. Civil Affairs team in Herat Province soon learned that local villagers had little or no contact with government authorities. Officials did not visit the villages, and the rural population held minimal expectations of services from provincial or Kabul-based officials. Many of the villagers were more accustomed to non-government organizations (NGOs) providing occasional services and development projects rather than the Afghan government's doing so. Unlike the United States, where citizens pay taxes and vocally express demands for services because they are taxpayers, citizens of many less developed countries pay no income tax and thus have less sense of "ownership" of the government bureaucracy.

The corollary to how the populace feels about the government bureaucracy is how the senior official feels about the populace. Does the official have a real concept of public service, or is he in office solely to enrich himself and his friends? If the latter, then the advisor might have to tailor his advice to areas that are both in the U.S. government's interests and will also incidentally add to the official's personal wealth. Or perhaps the advisor may be forced to simply limit his mission to "Do no harm."

The Trap of Personally Identifying with Foreign Officials.

In many countries, especially those which are coming out of recent conflict, senior officials have controversial histories. War is never one-sided, and the official may have enemies with blood feuds against him as well as loyal friends. Both may be powerful, and identification and companionship with the official will necessarily reflect on his American advisor. This means that the American advisor may inherit friends and enemies whom he has never met, giving him both entrée as well as putting barriers in front of him.

Any intelligent official—especially a shrewd and sly one—will make use of his American advisor as a scapegoat for his own misdeeds and mistakes, claiming that assignments, appointments, or allocation of resources are being forced on him by the American. The official will do so on the assumption that the American advisor will (1) never find out; or (2) will only be in country for a limited time, and can carry the onus of the senior official's mistakes out with him when he departs.

The official's claims that his hands are tied by the American advisor can make perfect local logic for a foreign populace that only sees the American advisor from a distance, regards the United States as a source of wealth and power, and is imbued with conspiracy theories that define foreigners as responsible for all evil that befalls their nation. The advisor will have to find local sources—perhaps a friend willing to be frank with him, perhaps his interpreter or other colleagues — who can keep him informed of what the official is claiming, and how others view the advisor and the minister.

On the other hand, the senior official might use his relationship with his American advisor to enhance his personal power. The advisor might be misused to inadvertently channel U.S. government-supplied resources to the official's friends, to recommend courses of action that will directly benefit the official, or even be misled by the official's slanted information to attack his enemies for him because they are allegedly "terrorists." The official might strengthen his power base by claiming to have personal support from "the Americans" or the international community, a claim that can have great resonance in a cash-strapped country that needs U.S. government assistance. Since the senior official will undoubtedly have higher political ambition, he can misuse the advisor's presence to imply that he has direct support from America, and thus build himself up at the expense of rivals who do not have American or other international advisors to enhance their prestige.

There are, of course, corollaries to this cycle of "use." If the American advisor has no resources or tangible benefits to offer the foreign official, he may be regarded as useless and simply discarded or isolated. If the foreign official seems to be reaping too much benefit from his association with the advisor, he may develop a reputation for being corrupt and "on the take" from foreign interests. If the senior official blames too much on the American, his own compatriots may start to view the official as weak and powerless.

Just as hostages sometimes display symptoms of the "Stockholm Syndrome" and begin to identify and sympathize with their captors, some advisors begin to identify with the ambitions of personable foreign officials. It is not the American advisor's role to help the official gain higher office or more power. Trying to groom the senior official for advancement is very likely to earn the Ambassador's displeasure or the unwanted attention of the official's own boss. While many American officers have tried to dabble in local politics by selecting a nominee for advancement, they rarely do it with full knowledge of his attributes or full understanding of the potential consequences. The results can be disastrous.

In a world very different from what is familiar to the American, and in a confusing, complex, and volatile environment, a local source who can provide meaning and structure to otherwise bewildering events and practices can be seized upon as a cultural life preserver. However, if the single-source's interpretation is flawed, self-serving, speculative, or simply nonfactual, the American advisor's credibility and effectiveness will suffer. For this reason the advisor must always avoid becoming too reliant on his counterpart's — or any other single source's — explanation of events or on his information. The advisor must take care to obtain his own advice and information about local conditions from multiple sources, to listen more than he talks, and to make final judgments with all due deliberation.

At the other extreme of possible advisor-senior official relationships, there are foreign officials who are so incompetent, so corrupt, or so personally unpleasant that working with them in an advisory capacity may simply be impossible. Dealing with this situation is difficult and sensitive, requiring serious consultation with the U.S. military command and the Embassy. There are no black and white rules for these situations, and much depends on the individuals involved. In the end, however, it is counterproductive to remain in a relationship which is so sour that the American advisor is ignored, disregarded, or seriously misused. Breaking the relationship with U.S. mission concurrence is not a sign of failure on the advisor's part, but a sign of good sense.

VII. OTHER PLAYERS ON THE FIELD

In any country where there is an American military officer assigned to advise a senior foreign official, there is certain to be a large number of individuals, offices, agencies, and organizations, both foreign and domestic, which will also have an interest or a need to influence and advise the same official. Some will be hostile to the American advisor and some will be friendly and cooperative, but each one will have his own agenda. These include the American Embassy, other embassies and international organizations, NGOs, the foreign and domestic media, and local interest groups covering a wide spectrum.

The U.S. Government Writ Large.

In addition to his own U.S. military organization in the country, the advisor may have to deal with various members of the American Embassy's Country Team or any number of American representatives. In many cases, these organizations' functions will be carried out by contractors who are hired to implement development programs, and perform specific training, logistics, or advisory functions. These implementers may include such private U.S. firms as Research Triangle, Inc., the Academy for Educational Development, Bearing Point, etc., as well as American NGOs, which may or may not have U.S. government funding. Private security firms such as Blackwater, Dyncorp, and many others are used extensively, especially in conflict regions. The list of contractor companies who may be dealing with the central government, or with a Cabinet member or Governor, is almost endless. Visitors from Congress (CODELs and STAFFDELs) will undoubtedly meet with the senior official as well. All of these organizations, companies, and groups will have an impact on senior foreign officials and their offices.

Every American who deals with him will regard the senior official in a slightly different light, and conflicts may arise within the official U.S. government community's perception of the foreign official which will directly affect on the advisor's mission. Except for the conduct of military operations, the senior American official in-country will always be the Ambassador, who directly represents the President of the United States. In general, the senior official with whom the advisor deals may also be routinely meeting with the American Ambassador or other members of the Country Team (see below), and the advisor may never learn what is discussed in private between the Ambassador and the senior official. The advisor must understand that the Ambassador's word is the final one, and that the Ambassador sets American policy towards the official and his ministry.

Various other Americans may see the senior official less often than the advisor does, but if they are directly providing financial assistance to him or are perceived as trusted and discreet partners, they may have far more influence than the military advisor. USAID, for example, will be involved with nation-state building programs such as democracy and governance, elections, civil-society development, and construction and development projects that affect the official's regional base of power or his personal prosperity, and thus also have influence with him.

In general, it is very conceivable that various other American government actors will have different agendas than the military advisor, and it is in his interests to know all the official American actors in the area; and, to the extent possible, cooperate with them in dealing with the senior official.

The Country Team.

Every American Embassy has a Country Team, composed of senior American staff of the various U.S. government agencies and military units represented in the Embassy. An advisor will probably not be a member of the Country Team, but he will certainly be called on to brief officials who are, and he will also routinely report through his chain of command to senior military officers who are members.

In theory, the Country Team meetings or smaller gatherings chaired by the Ambassador or his Deputy Chief of Mission (DCM) will determine and/or articulate U.S. government policy which may directly affect the senior official with whom the advisor works. In fact, there are often wheels within wheels, and competing agendas and agency interests are carried out by members of the Country Team who represent different U.S. government agencies. The advisor must establish a working relationship with the members of the Country Team, but must be aware that he will not always receive assistance, full disclosure, or cooperation from all members of the Country Team.

Misunderstandings and problems in cooperation can easily occur where there is a communications gap or when U.S. advisors or maneuver forces do not understand that their actions can impact negatively on overall American policy. For example, in a recent incident in Afghanistan, the residence compound of a very senior Member of Parliament with close ties to the American Embassy was raided by Afghan security forces who were accompanied by American security advisors. The consequence was an uproar in Parliament, hostile media reaction, and a feeling within the Afghan political structure that American policy was inconsistent and confused.

Other International Players.

Conditions change from country to country, but it is certain that some combination of international agencies and advisors will also be dealing with and trying to influence the senior official. The United Nations (UN) may have a significant presence in the host country, and the UN is composed of a wide variety of different agencies. International organizations like the Red Cross and the World Food Program may be very active, and there are certain to be a number of NGOs that are in-country. Other countries will have embassies and visiting delegations that affect the senior official's decisionmaking as well.

If the number of such organizations, agencies, NGOs, and all of their employees, contractors, and advisors were limited and cooperative, and if they had a single agenda, the advisor's life would be a simple one. The reality, however, is that there may be myriad foreign disparate groups, offices, and individuals, all with some claim to legitimacy and resources, that want to influence the senior official in different ways. What is absolutely certain is that some — or many — of these entities will be hostile to the American advisor's presence. Also certain is that some of these will have much better access — even if it is hidden from view — to the official than his American advisor will.

The Domestic Constituency.

"All politics are local." No matter what the American advisor says or does, it is still the domestic constituency which has the greatest impact on the senior official's decisionmaking, and the advisor's best recommendations will only be applied if they happen to coincide with the goals and interests of the official's local supporters. The advisor must know who the official's constituency is and where its interests lie.

Ultimately the senior official will have to serve both the interests of his own country and respond to his local constituency. When the advisor, the American military commander and the Ambassador are long-gone, the local constituency will still be there. The senior official's relationship with this constituency is likely to be more intense than would be the case for an American or other western official, with personal security and even his life depending on it.

The local constituency may be a general regional populace, a collection of ex-commanders and soldiers from the same side of the country's last war, a religious group, a business consortium, the local version of the Mafia, or the members of a particular family clan, but this is the group to whom the official owes final allegiance if he is to survive and to whom he is accountable.

The Media.

The advisor should not shy away from the media. Journalists and cameras will be omnipresent around a senior leader, and can be useful and positive factors in the advisor's mission.

Local and foreign media are certain to note the advisor's presence, and their reaction to it will vary from the positive to the poisonous. Even the American media will view the advisor's role in different ways, and he can envision publicity that might not be acceptable for viewing on the Armed Forces Network. However low key or discreet the advisor may be, details of his record and his activities will now be in the public realm and thus subject to question. This is not a matter of choice on the advisor's part, but simply a reality. Media attention on the advisor will also be affected by the importance and performance of the senior official he is advising.

Media outreach by the advisor, on the other hand, can be a very useful tool in his mission. If a public affairs officer is attached to the team of advisors, so much the better. Positive outreach can forestall criticism, explain issues and problems, and provide a realistic picture of progress and goals to the public, all of which enhance the chances of a successful advisory mission.

Unless the advisor is located on a secure base or in a controlled-access facility, the media may have full access to his work area, and may be closely following the daily activities of the senior official he is advising. Ignoring the media or trying to brush them off is usually not an option and will only make them portray the advisor's role in a negative way.

At a minimum, the advisor should establish a good relationship with both embassy and military Public Affairs officers. They are professionals who know the ins and outs of media relations and can offer guidance, expertise, and information that will help the advisor. Using their guidance and advice, the advisor should also establish a personal relationship with appropriate media representatives who can serve as a source of information and support in their own right. Local or international journalists can be excellent resources for the advisor to learn more about his counterpart senior official, pointing out aspects of the official's past or present behavior that explain his actions, and giving a heads up on political minefields that may pose challenges to the advisor's role.

Most importantly, however, the advisor must follow Country Team and military command guidelines in any contact with media. Facing a camera is not the time to freelance.

VIII. MILITARY ASSISTANCE AVAILABLE TO THE ADVISOR

There are resources available from the Department of Defense and Department of State to assist the advisor's mission. In many cases these resources will be crucial for the advisor's mobility and his ability to function in a country with a collapsing infrastructure. However, if he is not wearing a uniform and not directly attached to a military unit, obtaining these services can be a complex and frustrating process within the military system. Even if the advisor wears a uniform, attempting to obtain assistance from the local U.S. Embassy can bring him face to face with obstacles which may be more civilly presented but equally frustrating.

Essential Services.

In order to be effective, the advisor must have reliable transportation that will allow him to move freely to ministerial, regional, or provincial offices, to meeting locations, and even to areas across the country that the foreign official would like to visit. The advisor may lose face if he is late to meetings or cannot be present due to transportation issues. The military possesses numerous tactical vehicles, but these require a trained and licensed operator and often require a force protection component to travel away from the Forward Operating Base. Depending on the situation, this type of transportation may be the only option available and will require significant coordination to ensure that transportation is arranged on time. Due to the advisor's critical role, this bureaucracy can sometimes be mitigated by coordinating requirements with the military hierarchy. Leasing civilian vehicles which are more in keeping with the vehicles driven by the local population may be a possibility. One of these vehicles could be assigned to the advisor and should belong exclusively to him or the advisory team.

Local conditions are not always peaceful and may require the advisor to move through an unsafe area. In these situations, the advisor should be familiar with the rules for requesting force protection. This will normally entail the assignment of a group of armed military personnel to escort the advisor to his work place and remain in the vicinity until the advisor finishes his duties. The procedures to request this support can be time consuming and should be coordinated well in advance with the base defense operations center or the base military police. Another consideration involves the impact of this force on the foreign official's perceptions and his willingness to continue to invite the advisor into his office or compound. In some cases, the foreign official may view an armed American presence as an occupation force, placing him at risk because of his collaboration with foreign military forces.

Radios and cell phones are essential for the advisor's tasks and are typically plentiful. They allow him to relay information from the foreign official and can be a visible sign of the advisor's importance and usefulness if it allows him to keep his counterpart in touch with foreign VIPs. The advisor should take care to always have extra batteries, a charger that works on the local electrical current, and an appropriate number of payment cards. All of these can be typically obtained from the military communications or logistics officers. Lacking the ability to communicate externally at a moment's notice will diminish the advisor's usefulness and affect his mission. Cell phones can frequently be out of range, so radios are important to provide quick connectivity to security forces when travelling to and from the foreign official's workplace, to the locations of external meetings, and to visits in other provinces or regions.

*****

During Operation ENDURING FREEDOM, cell phone cards, which provided a quantifiable number of minutes, were in great demand. Although the cards could be commonly purchased on the streets of Afghanistan and there was apparently no shortage of them, within the U.S. military a rationing system was implemented. Under this system, various sections received a different quantity of cell phone cards each month. Without available minutes, cell phones were useless. Toward the end of the month, soldiers could be found going from office to office looking for spare cards to provide them an extra hour or two of cell phone coverage. For the astute advisor, one of the greatest rewards that could be given to a young Afghan policeman or soldier was a 20-minute "Roshan card."

*****

Another asset available to advisors is a plethora of country studies and intelligence, both unclassified and classified. Information available typically includes population studies, ethnographic studies, terrain studies, key personnel assessments, and reports from military units operating in the area. Other assets include studies about senior foreign officials developed by various agencies. This information is especially crucial as it may clarify what makes a foreign official "tick." Such reports are difficult to access, but they are available and will help the advisor develop an understanding of the terrain. Information of this nature can be obtained from both the military headquarters and from the local U.S. Embassy. A wise advisor should seek out the military intelligence officer or Defense Attaché at the Embassy, explain his upcoming task, and ask for all information that is available.

Common to military operations is a component of civilian contractors who are hired to provide continuity during enduring operations. These individuals act across the operational continuum, and the duration of their contract will often exceed the duration of the advisor's assignment. Their personal knowledge and tendency to document their work plans, goals, and accomplishments can provide the advisor with a wealth of information. Many of the contractors working to establish institutional processes and functionality are required to maintain long-term, detailed plans which delineate a series of quantifiable objectives, and these are often tied to one-on-one interactions with foreign officials and large forum meetings. Tapping into the knowledge and written products maintained by U.S. government contractors will help to educate the advisor on what has been done previously, on future projects that may directly involve the senior foreign official, and on potential future contacts that the advisor can help to coordinate.

Military bases offer a significant number of facilities and services, to include meeting rooms and dining facilities. After establishing his relationship with the senior foreign official, it can be useful to invite him to the base and host him for a meal in conjunction with a meeting. However, there are numerous pitfalls to avoid in such hospitality. These include ensuring that the official is not subjected to security screening, making certain his vehicles are allowed onto the compound or base, and arranging a welcome by an appropriate level of official. A photographer should be present to document the event, and the foreign official should be invited to speak first at the meeting. Refreshments and food should be culturally appropriate. A reliable and proficient interpreter must be present, even if the official speaks English, because many foreign VIPs will insist on speaking their own language at a formal or public event. Based upon the facilities and support available, an American military base may also be a logical location to hold meetings with other parties and agencies who influence the foreign official. However, the advisor must always avoid being seen as arrogant or expecting other parties to come to him, balancing the use of American facilities against the potential negative perception.

Personal Risk: A Cost-Benefit Analysis.

Although personal safety is important, the wearing of protective gear and the requirement to be armed warrant discussion. An advisor entering a foreign official's office with a Kevlar helmet, body armor, and a weapon will transmit the wrong message to a local official dressed in traditional clothing or a western suit and tie. If the advisor participates in meetings in such battle gear, it will provoke an even more negative reaction, and is likely to negate his ability to influence anyone. In Afghanistan, for example, foreign soldiers who come armed and in full protective gear to civilian events are often regarded as cowards by the local populace. Ultimately, the advisor must weigh the risks against the benefits, determine his own level of comfort, and then dispense with personal protective gear inside the workplace. The advisor should also consider wearing civilian clothes in place of a uniform, especially in an office setting.

Traveling with a senior foreign official is another situation requiring consideration. If the advisor is asked to travel in host nation transportation and instead insists on using American military vehicles, he may be disinvited, because the foreign official can determine that he is at greater risk by including readily recognizable military assets in his delegation. The advisor should consult with his military and civilian chain of command to determine the feasibility of travelling with a foreign official and only using host nation support. If an advisor travels in a heavily armored SUV while the rest of the party is using normal sedans, it sends the message that he is afraid of his surroundings, or does not trust the official and other members of the local entourage.

IX. PREPARATION AND COORDINATION — APPROACHING THE JOB

The advisor's best weapon is knowledge, and gaining proficiency starts with the day he learns of his assignment and continues until his departure from the position. Knowing the facts about the country, the legal framework for his own presence, and meeting the people who will support his mission are all essential as he begins his duties. He should go forward steadily and with patience, always remembering that the advisory role is not a zero-sum game, but a process of shaping both the senior foreign official as well as the advisor in order to help both do a better job.

The Preparation Checklist.

1. Develop Historical/Situational Awareness of the Country. Query academic institutions, knowledge centers, trade journals, and government and international organizations. Look for books available on *Amazon.com*, and check the shelves at Borders and Barnes & Noble. Spend time on Google, Wikipedia, and the Internet in general. Useful sites include *www.amazon.com, www.barnesandnoble.com, www.state. gov, www.usaid.gov, www.cia.gov, www.defense.gov, www.smallwarsjournal.com, www.csis.org, www.usip.org, www.mideasti.org, www.carnegieendowment.org, www. wilsoncenter.org, www.brookings.edu, www.Strategic StudiesInstitute.army.mil, www.effectivestates.org, www. carlisle.army.mil/usawc/Parameters*, and many, many more.

2. Obtain Practical Knowledge of the Country. Read commonly available treaties and country studies, visit cultural portals, and talk to people previously assigned to the area. Search the embassy (both American and host country) websites of the country to which you are being assigned. (American embassy websites overseas can be accessed through *www.state.gov*, and foreign embassy websites can be obtained through a quick Google search.) Know how your own country and its history and institutions relate to the host country.

3. Develop and Employ Personal Contacts. Use officers at the U.S. Department of State, the military service war colleges, academic institutions, and think tanks to get advice and direction. Try to attend appropriate lectures and conferences sponsored by academic and government agencies, because one timely conference can introduce you to a network of people dealing with your country.

4. Understand Local and National Holidays. Understand the national importance of the country's holidays and their impact upon work. Remember the time-honored maxim of never arriving at your new post on a holiday. Learn which actions are appropriate to demonstrate a deeper understanding of local holidays (e.g., if, how, and when to send congratulatory messages).

5. Know and Understand U.S. and International Policy towards the Region. Contact Department of Defense and Department of State regional bureaus to obtain official policy guidance. Check the local U.S. Embassy website for the nation to which you will be deploying to access recent speeches.

6. Read Essential Documents. Read the host nation's constitution, and be familiar with the American constitution as well. Read any Status of Forces Agreements (SOFA) that explain the U.S. military presence. Study international (UN or NATO) declarations involving the intervention or situation within the nation. Read any treaties and agreements to which the host country is a signatory. Know the relevant strategic and policy documents which the host country and the United States have jointly produced or signed (bilateral agreements).

7. Be Conversant in the Local Governmental Structure. Understand the type of government and its basic structure. Study the structure of the specific ministry to which you are assigned.

8. Know the Basics of the Language. "Hello, goodbye, thank you, yes, no" — the basic terms of politeness — are mandatory. Learn one or two new words every day.

9. Recognize Nonverbal Communication. Learn the physical signals and gestures that convey meaning in the local culture, and stop using American gestures that send unwanted meanings.

10. Understand and Apply Cultural Knowledge. Learn the basic etiquette that is used locally. Identify a colleague, interpreter, or local friend who can guide you on points of etiquette and culture.

11. Seek Knowledge from Your Predecessor. Contact the person you are replacing. Determine what preparations can be made to make transition easier on both sides.

12. Research the Foreign Official. Learn the name of the person you will be advising. Do a name search on Google. Read any articles about him and anything that he has written. Coordinate with appropriate agencies to get a briefing on him.

13. Understand the U.S. Command Structure. Learn who you will work for while serving as an advisor. Contact this individual(s), and identify any issues and agendas prior to deploying. Schedule a meeting with him as soon as possible when you arrive in country.

14. Understand the Key Individuals in the Chain of Command. Immediately after arrival at your post, schedule meetings to introduce yourself at the U.S. Embassy (Office Directors, Deputy Chief of Mission, and even the Ambassador), Military Headquarters (Commanding General), or International Assistance Mission Headquarters (Special Envoys, others).

15. Coordinate In-country Logistics Support. The Embassy or military unit will have its own check-in list, but be certain to include the following:
- Arranging daily transportation;
- Cell phones/radios/chargers;
- 24/7 contact information of the interpreter;
- Force protection; and,
- Key personnel contact numbers.

16. Meet Your Interpreter. Before you begin to use him as a translator, spend a significant amount of time, one on one, understanding this individual. Make sure he understands you.

17. The Current Advisor. Spend as much time as possible with him in order to learn procedures and practices that have worked in the past, things to avoid, office practices, and other helpful information.

18. Ask For an Introductory Meeting with the Foreign Official. This should be a long session that the departing advisor attends. Discuss his departure timing, and when you will assume your responsibilities. Be certain the senior official agrees to the timing.

19. Observe the Current Status Quo. Shadow the current advisor and simply watch what he does. Observe office protocol and best business practices.

20. Take Charge. Establish a transition date and when you will assume your primary duties. The previous advisor should not interact with the foreign official once you have taken charge.

X. DEPARTING THE COUNTRY

The advisor's main goal should be to work himself out of a job and make the advisory role unnecessary in the country. By passing his experience on to a successor and, more importantly, to local leaders, he improves his chance of a successful mission.

A good advisor is both a teacher and a student. His relationship with a foreign official may — or may not — result in influencing the official to act in ways that will benefit both the country of assignment and the United States. At the very least, however, it is an educational process for the advisor himself, and he will leave his post with a much greater appreciation for a different culture and a different military and political reality. This provides immediate benefit for him, his chain of command, and the overall interests of the U.S. government.

Every assignment comes to an end, some according to a time line that simply ordains the number of months in advance, some when a project is complete, some when circumstance — wars, changes in national policy — no longer permit an American to remain at his posting. While the period of time spent at an assignment is by no means the only factor for evaluating the advisor's success, it is an important one. Becoming familiar and confident in the environment, developing personal relationships with the senior official and those around him, watching the seeds of an idea germinate in the new environment, knowing that one's ideas and advice are being tested and applied — all these are difficult to measure by standard metrics or to regulate by routine assignment procedures.

A major part of the advisor's departure is preparing the way for his successor. Because the assignment bureaucracy can be impersonal and remote, he must stress to his leadership the date of his departure to ensure that his successor is identified and provided a period of training and overlap in order to effect a seamless transition. Records, accomplishments, failures, a wish list, and as much information as possible should be passed to the incoming advisor and his team. A senior official from the Presidential Palace noted that not doing this was a consistent failure of foreign advisors departing Kabul.

There are ways to prepare a successor. If there is a full advisory team, departure dates can be staggered to ensure that the new personnel have time to learn their duties while some members of the old team are still in place and available for guidance. This is especially important for the head of the team and his deputy, and consideration should be given to having staggered assignments so that one or two of the top echelon of advisors remain to serve with the new team. Email contact between an advisor and his successor well in advance of departure is important and fairly easy, and every effort should be made to prevent gaps in the advisory presence.

The advisor should leave time for farewells. To depart precipitously will be an insult to his foreign colleagues and friends and place his successor in an awkward position. Even after leaving, he should remember to maintain social contact with friends and colleagues, but in a way that does not detract from his successor's official role. Today's foreign Governor or Colonel can be tomorrow's Head of State or Minister of Defense, and the relationship will bear fruit in the future.

As he analyzes his own performance, the advisor should not be overly harsh on himself. His duty, after all, is to advise and consult, and not to be a colonial administrator. The advisor cannot—and should not—do "everything." That is the responsibility of the country's officials and citizens, not the American officer. The advisor must always remember that he can make a significant and long-lasting contribution, however, and that there is great value in his efforts for both the United States and the host country. His advice may save American and host country lives, improve living conditions for many people, and foster good relations and a more hopeful future for both countries.

In the end, the personal nature of the advisory relationship will also affect the assignment timetable. An advisor should stay long enough to have an impact, but from the beginning must try to do his job well enough to make himself unnecessary and dispensable. Influencing and advising the foreign official to the point where he no longer needs an American advisor is the true mark of success.

ENDNOTES

1. Lieutenant Colonel Mark Grdovic, "The Advisory Challenge," *Special Warfare*, January-February 2008, p. 23.

2. Edward C. Stuart, "American Advisors Overseas," *Military Review*, February 1965. Cited in Robert D. Ramsey III, *Advice for Advisors: Suggestions and Observations from Lawrence to the Present*, Combat Studies Institute Occasional Paper, GWOT OP#19, Ft. Leavenworth, KS: Combat Studies Institute Press, 2006, p. 17.

3. *Ibid.*, p. 23.

www.ingramcontent.com/pod-product-compliance
Lightning Source LLC
Chambersburg PA
CBHW031259280526
45784CB00004B/1914